FLORISTS' REVIEW

Christmas
traditions

FLORISTS' REVIEW

Christmas

traditions

A treasury of floral decorations for the holidays

PUBLISHER
Frances Dudley

EXECUTIVE EDITOR
Talmage McLaurin, AIFD

FLORAL DESIGNERS
Talmage McLaurin, AIFD
James Miller, AIFD
BIll Harper, AIFD, AAF
Phil Marvin

AUTHORS
David Coake
Shelley Urban

ART DIRECTOR
Holly Foster

PRODUCTION COORDINATOR
James Miller, AIFD

PHOTOGRAPHERS
Stephen Smith
Mark Robbins

Christmas Traditions is published by
Florists' Review Enterprises, Topeka,
Kansas. www.floristsreview.com

Printed in the United States by
Mainline Printing, Topeka, Kansas.

ISBN 0-9714860-4-2

Florists Review is the only independent
monthly trade magazine for professional
florists in the United States. In addition
to serving the needs of retail florists
through its industry-specific magazine,
Florists' Review Enterprises has an active
book division that supplies educational
products to all who are interested in floral
design. For more information, visit our
Web site at www.floristsreview.com.

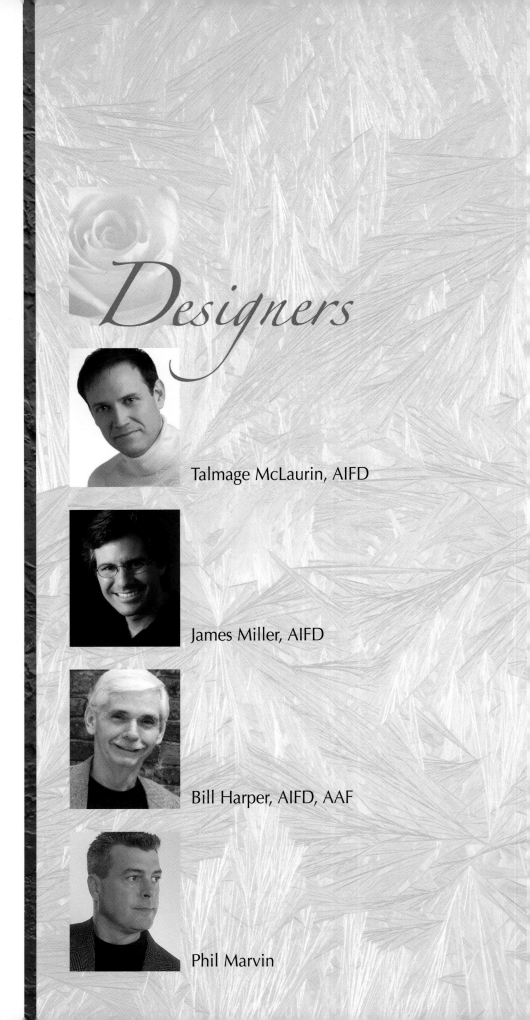

Designers

Talmage McLaurin, AIFD

James Miller, AIFD

Bill Harper, AIFD, AAF

Phil Marvin

Introduction

Each year *Florists Review* magazine starts celebrating Christmas in July with our preview of floral and decorating trends for the holidays. We continue our coverage through December knowing that, for Americans, the Christmas season is the most celebrated of all seasons.

Over the past eight years, since our first Christmas book, we have continued to collect ideas and images that celebrate the many color stories, personalities, and themes that enhance this much-loved celebration.

And it's again time to share the collective wealth of our Christmases past – full of decorations, designs, tips, techniques, and, of course, our popular how-to's that allow for each project to be easily and professionally reproduced.

Christmas Traditions is truly a treasury of inspiration, brimming with the very joy and excitement that makes the holidays the most wonderful time of the year.

Contents

Classic Red

STEPHEN SMITH

OPPOSITE PAGE Among many sentimental collectibles are ruby-colored crystal vases, bowls, glasses and goblets, many of which are sparklingly illuminated from within by votive candles. Here, an assortment of ruby glass pieces surrounds a mounded centerpiece of herbs and velvety-red 'Charlotte' roses and adds a touch of elegance to the informal dining table.

ABOVE & LEFT Straight-sided glass votive candleholders are perfect for wrapping with a variety of ribbons and creating one-of-a-kind accessories for holiday decorating or parties. These votive holders are just the right height for #40-width ribbons, which are applied with heavy-duty spray adhesive.

OPPOSITE PAGE In each of these oversized, gobletlike containers, branches of flat cedar are placed to curve around the interior of the glass, partially but artfully obscuring a large red-and-green-banded pillar candle that is stabilized in white aquarium gravel. Completing the holiday adornment, like fabulous bows on special gifts, a mix of fabric flowers, permanent berries, fresh pine, and pine cones adorns the goblets' stems.

RIGHT 'Forever Young' roses, noble fir, and frosted glass millimeter balls come together for a traditional Christmas look of red and green. A low bowl filled with fresh floral foam is the base of the creation, which is more of an arrangement than a traditional candle ring. The candle is placed on the foam first, and the fresh materials are arranged around it.

OPPOSITE PAGE The traditional Christmas colors of red and hunter green receive antique gold accents with this plaid ribbon that is wrapped around a 10-inch-tall column candle in a pot. Holly, evergreen, and a red cardinal also evoke the Christmas sentiment. The cardinal is perched on a branch that is inserted into a hole made in the side of the candle with a heated ice pick. This design makes a wonderful addition to holiday tabletops.

LEFT A luscious mound of Christmas red carnations and a red pillar candle, which are placed into rustic faux moss-covered pots, receive a simple holiday treatment with a few sprigs of distinctive curly pine *(Calothamnus)*. As a set or individually, these quick and easy holiday accessories are great for both giftgiving and home decorating.

In the center of a buffet is a 1940s-era cookie jar Santa that is filled with a gardeny arrangement of Christmassy-red 'Charlotte' roses and assorted conifers. The cookie jar rests in the center of a coordinating wreath arrangement and is flanked by a replica Thomas Nash Santa and a toby mug.

RIGHT These decorative tin gift bags, which come painted red and rubbed for an aged look, are charming containers for a variety of uses including clever holiday arrangements, Christmas card holders, wall hangings, and more. Here, peppermint carnations, miniature red carnations, and noble fir, which are placed individually into water picks, are accented with frosted glass millimeter balls. To arrange the fresh materials, insert the water picks into a 1-inch-thick piece of dry foam inside each bag.

STEPHEN SMITH

STEPHEN SMITH

LEFT Many items of giftware have crossover appeal, such as this heart-shaped red tin wall basket, which, when filled with fresh sweetheart roses in water tubes and hung on a tree, becomes an enchanting Christmas ornament.

Tailored bow "wreaths," fashioned from holly print fabric ribbon, accent a ginger jar and a cylinder vase. The ginger jar contains a bouquet of 'Charlotte' roses, and the vase displays a single rose that appears to float, with its stem length matching the water depth. Lily grass repeats the circular pattern. Two cardboard discs are covered in crisscross fashion with the holly-patterned ribbon as well as the red satin ribbon to carry the effect underneath.

how-to
ribbon wreaths for vases

(see opposite page)

Cut a small wreath-shaped
form from a piece of
cardboard, and wrap it
with ribbon.

Fold a two-loop bow with
streamers, and hot-glue it
to the ribbon-wrapped ring.

Slide each wreath over the
top of a vase, and arrange
florals into the vase.

MARK ROBBINS

Composed of weatherproof
products, this wreath will
resist the hazards of the
season and remain intact
and looking great throughout
the holidays.

19

how-to
poinsettia appliqués

Cut out two poinsettias from a length of printed ribbon.

Spray adhesive on the backs of the ribbon poinsettias.

Press the ribbon poinsettias onto a vase.

STEPHEN SMITH

Exquisite designs abound when it comes to holiday ribbons, and when carefully cut out, they can become lovely appliqués for all sorts of floral projects. Here, festive glittered poinsettias are cut out and adhered to a frosted glass vase, creating a custom Christmas container.

This pair of pillar candle designs, created by placing the chunky candles atop floral foam inside mint julep containers, couldn't be easier and more time-efficient to create. Yet, despite their easy assembly, they couldn't be more stunning. To accentuate the deep red tones in the candles, powdery white snowberries (*Symphoricarpos*) along with sprigs of fir are tucked into the foam around the candles' bases.

how-to
ribbon-covered cone

STEPHEN SMITH

Wrap a plastic foam cone in a spiral manner with tapestry ribbon, and secure in place with greening pins. Add pieces of ribbon with scrolled ends as decorative flourishes.

Invert the cone, and attach a hanger fashioned of wired gold twine or cord to the wide end of the cone with greening pins and hot glue.

STEPHEN SMITH

ABOVE Ornate velvet ribbon glittered with gold is glued onto a cone, with a few scrolled pieces spiraling down, creating a Victorian effect. Permanent roses and holly leaves accent the cone. In the tradition of the era that inspired this design, it would work well on a Christmas tree as an ornament, hanging from a doorknob, or hanging from a wall sconce.

Arrange permanent florals into the top end of the cone, and add a tassel-like finish made with a cluster of holly leaves at the bottom point.

RIGHT Opulent antique silver and crystal accessories dominate a formal dining setting. The floral materials are simply accents to the silver and crystal: a wreath of crimson 'Charlotte' roses and other texturally interesting botanicals surrounds a mirrored plateau on which a resplendent candelabrum, circa 1880, reigns over the table; an orb of roses completes a silver bridal basket.

STEPHEN SMITH

Ordinary 3-inch-diameter plastic foam balls become subtly extravagant holiday ornaments when wrapped with layers of luxurious hand-dyed silk ribbons. Such exquisite handcrafted decoratives are generally found at fine specialty boutiques and can command nice prices, but now, you can make your own.

STEPHEN SMITH

STEPHEN SMITH

how-to
ribbon ornaments
(see opposite page)

Insert two pins into a plastic foam ball at the axis points. Holding both pins, spin the ball to make sure that the pins are in exactly the right spots.

Wrap the ball with ribbon beginning at one "pole," or pin, and passing to the opposite pole, around the pin, with each wrap. Twist the ribbon at each pole, and overlap the edges slightly as you proceed.

When the ball is covered, secure the ribbon with the pin, and cut the end short. For the tie, thread a piece of ribbon underneath one of the layers of ribbon, and secure it in place at the nearest pole with a knot.

how-to
stacked package tree

Cover cardboard craft boxes with permanent rose petals, leaves, and mossed paper using spray adhesive.

Stack the covered boxes, from largest to smallest, forming a tree shape. Enhance the tree with fabric roses and ribbons.

Set tiered packages on a coordinating urn, and create a tree topper from a miniature urn and covered foam sphere.

The season of giving is perfectly celebrated with this tree, which is formed by stacking gift boxes on top of a stone urn. Permanent and preserved foliages, in various shades of green, are attached to the boxes and lids with spray adhesive. Red ribbon and velvet rose petals add splashes of color to the design. The crowning glory of this tree is the miniature arrangement on top, containing an ivy-covered sphere and pretty velvet roses in a tiny urn.

STEPHEN SMITH

This classical-form tree is bursting with the brilliant colors of the season. Permanent ivy leaves are attached to a foam sphere and cone with spray adhesive. The tree shape is then decorated with holly, crisp red ribbon, and more ivy. A simple urn forms the base for this architectural design.

Evergreen

Lichen-covered round and conical forms, available readymade, are the foundations of these topiarylike creations. Gold, plastic foam ornaments on picks, carefully coordinated with the pots, are used as decorative toppers and "trunks." As is, they're elegant in their simplicity, or for those who desire more adornment, they're ripe for further decoration.

STEPHEN SMITH

how-to
galax christmas tree

Spray stemless *Galax* leaves with adhesive, and cover a floral foam cone, leaving the plastic covering intact.

When the cone is covered with overlapping leaves, wrap the surface of the cone with silver bullion.

Attach the cone to a custom-made base.

These glamorous Christmas accessories are made by layering *Galax* leaves onto floral foam cones. The leaves are attached to the cones' plastic wrapping with spray adhesive, and wrappings of silver bullion add a shimmery holiday feel to the designs.

Each silver tree stand comprises a candleholder and a small clay pot. Satin cord is wrapped around the base of each pot and accented with a button cover. Each stand is then sprayed with silver paint.

RIGHT Combinations of fruit and foliage are a natural for centerpiece decorations. Bowls of fruit used as functional and edible displays show up historically on Victorian tables as well as in early American Colonial designs. Today, especially around the holidays, it's almost impossible to pick up a shelter magazine without finding the fruit-and-flower or fruit-and-foliage combination. Here, 'Granny Smith' apples, on wooden picks, are arranged among various pines and huckleberry.

STEPHEN SMITH

LEFT A definite holiday showstopper, this design is as easy to make as it is dramatic. Extraordinary feather-covered cones are casually and securely placed inside an iron urn, then filled with snips of ivy in water tubes and topped with an *Echeveria*. Because it is a succulent, the *Echeveria* needs no water supply and will last beautifully.

STEPHEN SMITH

A new twist in bubble-bowl presentations is evident in this fun, easy-to-create centerpiece composed of sliced limes and lime-hued 'Lady Green' carnations. Because the materials are submersed, the use of flower food solution is recommended to prevent bacterial growth. This specialty design is especially fun and eye-catching for holiday party tables.

OPPOSITE PAGE With a captivating selection of fresh materials, this traditionally styled design sparks new excitement for the holidays. The foliage materials that compose the framework and extremities of the design include yellow-green *Leucadendron laureoleum,* *Grevillea* 'Ivanhoe,' summer myrtle *(Melaleuca nesaphila),* and holiday sumac *(Rhus).* Brownish-burgundy *Hypericum* fruit, treated with leaf shine for added gloss, is arranged in mass, forming the heart of the arrangement. Fragrant white stocks, the only "flowers" in the design, are placed intermittently around it.

LEFT A ready-made twig wreath forms the base of this simple and natural design in which permanent apples and holly, as well as clumps of dried moss, are attached with hot glue.

how-to
tree of bells

Cut stems of bells-of-Ireland into sections between clusters of florets.

Using pan-melt glue, attach a floral foam cone to a plastic-lined, foam-filled, painted clay pot.

Arrange the bells-of-Ireland sections to cover the foam cone, and add jingle bells and ribbon accents.

STEPHEN SMITH

Now anyone can have an elegant Christmas tree to decorate even the smallest of spaces. Covering a wet floral foam cone, the ruffly, eye-catching greenery of this holiday tree is actually individual florets plucked from bells-of-Ireland *(Moluccella)* stems. Oversized jingle bells, mounted on wood picks, add a festive touch to the holiday creation. Finishing off the petite tree are a jaunty gold bow fashioned from sheer mesh ribbon and a clay pot that is painted metallic gold.

Flames and foliages are safely combined in these pretty candlelit creations, which feature flat cedar affixed with spray adhesive to the outside of clear glass vases. Inside each milk-jug-style container, a layer of aquarium gravel helps secure a holiday-scented pillar candle.

STEPHEN SMITH

OPPOSITE PAGE Everyday glass vessels transcend their utilitarian function with creative yuletide enhancements. Inside, protected from any candlelight hazard, are mixes of traditional holiday elements such as fresh cedar, cones, nuts, and cinnamon sticks. Atop the vases, ball candles, in shades of green, are accessorized with wrappings of grapevine, crafted from disassembled miniature grapevine wreaths. The wrappings enable a successful visual transition from the organic materials within to the smooth orbs on top.

ABOVE These clever wooden "shingle" trees, with an informal, almost animated quality, would be outstanding atop a table in a country-theme room. Premade and ready to go out of the box, they need no additional decoration.

LEFT The small-leafed heath *Banksia* foliage *(B. ericafolia)* is ideal for this contemporary styling because of its flexible branches. Entwined around and secured with silver paddle wire to the top of a striking open-frame urn, the heath *Banksia* foliage provides a pinelike adornment to the urn, which, when filled with ornaments, becomes a sophisticated holiday decoration.

Frosted White

OPPOSITE PAGE Icy white is one of the coolest themes for the holiday season, and what is more familiar than wintry wonderland decorations and accessories? This updated scene features a contemporary swag comprising a variety of icy branches and two types of snowballs—both the throwing kind and the growing kind (*Viburnum*) as well as acrylic and silver-leaf deer. Crystal "ice-covered" trees, with a contemporary form, complete this modern adaptation.

LEFT Lending a contemporary character to any seasonal occasion, a splendid glass bowl, artfully filled with swirling callas and crushed glass, is sure to create plenty of wonderment and garner plenty of approval. The calla stems are held into place, under water, by the ice-cube-looking chunks of glass that fill the bowl and beckon to be dropped into a holiday cocktail. Ice crystal ornaments are the ideal accents to extend the personality of the design.

RIGHT Icons of American folk art, this two-dimensional wooden angel and the wooden peace dove combine perfectly with nature-inspired holiday decoratives such as the wood-toned foliage swag and sisal rope balls.

BELOW Reflecting the holiday appeal of primitive American art, a folk angel crafted from a finial doubles as a candleholder while unassuming hurricane vases contain collections of seasonal favorites.

STEPHEN SMITH

STEPHEN SMITH

OPPOSITE PAGE Christmas gets a "shabby chic" nod in this heavenly vignette featuring handcrafted and folk-artlike decoratives with whitewashed, weathered, and pickled finishes. Florals include whitewashed and gold-leafed drieds and bleached star flowers arranged in a gold-and-white, hand-lettered pot.

OPPOSITE PAGE The focus of this vignette is on using permanent flowers for Christmas that look surprisingly like fresh cut flowers. Christmas roses (*Helleboruses*), stars of Bethlehem, and hyacinths, all in white, exemplify this symbolic feeling. A Wardian case and a faux stone garden planter provide other gardeny additions while silver-toned vases and a wreath of permanent cedar reinforce the holiday ambience.

STEPHEN SMITH

STEPHEN SMITH

LEFT A parlorlike setting is styled with a naturally hued *Anaphalis* wreath and an overflowing table arrangement of cabbage roses, *Hydrangea* florets, and handcrafted glass Czechoslovakian ornaments.

how-to
wax-covered basket

Melt paraffin in a full-size electric skillet, which will allow you to adjust the temperature as needed.

Set the chosen wire basket into the skillet, and pour melted paraffin over the basket using a ladle.

Repeat the coating process several times until the desired thickness of paraffin is achieved. Let the paraffin cool between coatings.

STEPHEN SMITH

After a thorough drenching with melted paraffin, a wire-frame, Victorian-style basket looks as if it's made of ice-covered branches. Its frigid, almost-rustic character is ideal for this wintry collection of white *Hydrangeas*, *Scabiosas*, and pine cones, which is punctuated with sprigs of cedar, noble fir, and white pine. The floral materials are arranged in glass tubes that are dropped into the open-weave basket to mimic the look of icicles.

A wreath of sparkling crystal beads, placed around the neck of a sandstone-finish, plastic jardiniere, adds opulence to a mounded collection of winter white florals including 'Akito' roses, carnations, stars-of-Bethlehem (*Ornithogalum*) and loosestrife (*Lysimachia*). A lovely seasonal gift or party centerpiece, the arrangement is accented with a coordinating crystal angel, which adds to the holiday spirit.

A feeling of restrained opulence radiates from this collection of Victorian-inspired decoratives. Victorian angel figurines, miniature tabletop trees, heavily beaded and encrusted ornaments, and decorated eggs compose this display.

STEPHEN SMITH

LEFT A sumptuous orb of creamy roses (two varieties, 'Escimo' and 'Vendela,' are chosen for the depth their subtle color differences create) is flanked by a stemmed crystal urn topped with a luxuriant composition of white roses, green-and-white ivy, and evergreens that are designed on a crystal plate. Inside the urns, miniature environments are created with more roses along with berries and apples.

STEPHEN SMITH

LEFT Inspired by a formal, snow-covered hedgerow that's been left somewhat untended, this dense, detailed design, in an ornate but weathered rectangular planter box, features fresh 'Akito' roses that are arranged in three ordered rows and surrounded with snips of fresh pine, fir, and cedar. Accenting the "overgrown" border of conifers is a woodsy collection of pine cones, walnuts, permanent tallow berries, natural and permanent vines, fresh white button spray mums, and, for a dash of elegance, gold-painted wooden eggs.

STEPHEN SMITH

how-to
ranunculus pot

Place a bird's nest upside-down over a floral-foam-filled pot. Pierce the nest with a screwdriver for the flower stem. Arrange bits of foliage, berries, pine cones, and honeysuckle vine wreaths into the floral foam.

RIGHT In a weathered ceramic pot instead of a vase, a single white buttercup (*Ranunculus*) is nestled in a woodsy collection of twigs (actually an inverted twig bird's nest), honeysuckle vines, white snowberries (*Symphoricarpos*), green chinaberries (*Melia*), pine cones, and bits of hemlock (*Tsuga*) foliage, creating a miniature landscapelike presentation. This design idea is equally ideal for spotlighting other single flowers with a gardeny allure.

Reminiscent of the first bulblike flowers of spring peeking through the snow from a late-season storm, this nest full of lilies-of-the-valley (*Convallaria*) makes a sumptuous holiday presentation. Permanent tallow berries combined with fresh berried juniper create a wreathlike edging atop the bird's nest container, which is drizzled with paraffin to engender an ice-glazed feeling.

OPPOSITE PAGE A gathering of materials, some in wintry white and others in warm creamy hues, are highlighted with hints of gold in this classic urn arrangement that demonstrates the opulence of a bygone era. Like the urn, a pair of painted candlesticks show the patina of age.

ABOVE Classic earth tones dominate these natural holiday decoratives, which include a shell wreath and lichen-and-feather-covered spheres on ornate candlesticks. The same spheres, in graduated sizes, form a rustic topiary.

RIGHT Wrapping candles with bands of seasonal ribbon, can create "designer" looks from rustic to elegant. You can even transform everyday candles into seasonal specialties with the right ribbon, like these white pillars, which are customized with a formal, holly-patterned ribbon with wired edges. A silver fringe ribbon is tucked into the candleholders to add an extra touch of holiday sparkle.

STEPHEN SMITH

LEFT This frosty white candle design offers safe, refillable alternatives to traditional hurricane designs. By using hurricane and cylindrical vases filled with decorative gravel, votive candles are elevated to a safe distance above the flammable flowers and foliages. This assembly also allows votive candles to be replaced easily, frequently, and inexpensively.

STEPHEN SMITH

Spanning more than 2 feet in diameter, this sumptuous centerpiece of 'Million Stars' *Gypsophila*, with its white and silver color palette, has an ethereal quality that is appropriate for all winter celebrations. Arranged into a floral foam wreath form, *Gypsophila* is inserted in small clusters in two layers—one short and dense to cover the foam and one longer and airier to add dimension. Votive candles are placed onto the surface of the foam wreath before the *Gypsophila* is arranged, and a variety of silver ornaments adds holiday sparkle.

OPPOSITE PAGE A glitter-dusted green-and-white kale is the centerpiece of this centerpiece, which also comprises an assortment of green fresh fruits and foliages, white dried materials, and natural-colored branches and cones.

BELOW A not-so-traditional interpretation of the classic topiary form, this delightfully fragrant, ball-shaped bundle of paperwhites (*Narcissus*), bound with a chenille stem, rises above a Biedermeier-inspired arrangement of young *Narcissus* bulbs, clusters of bleached star flowers, and sprigs of *Oregonia*. The dusting of "snow" over the bulbs, achieved with opalescent glitter, and the matte-finish aluminum vase engender a wintry feeling. Lily grass (*Liriope*), woven and tucked in and around the "trunk" of the topiary, creates a sense of motion within the otherwise static design.

ABOVE When a wintry, woodsy ambience for a seasonal buffet is the goal, this expressive design will do the trick. In a bullet-shaped aluminum vase, an eclectic collection of fresh and dried materials is arranged in a modified traditional style. Composing a central triangular form are branches of silver fir; sprigs of *Oregonia* and seeded *Eucalyptus*; strands of lily grass (*Liriope*); white-pine cones; bleached star flowers; and fresh fruits, which are "frosted" with flat white paint and opalescent glitter. With the addition of fresh *Narcissi* and hawthorn, along with dried prairie grass and lambs' ears, increased dimension and a free-form style are created.

61

how-to
wax foliage cones
(see opposite page)

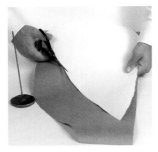

Cut a triangular shape from a piece of heavy kraft paper. Form it into a cone, and tape it into shape along the seam. Tape the paper cone onto an angled, spindle-like stand.

Using floral adhesive, glue stems of steel grass to the paper cone, with the narrow tips of the steel grass at the pointed end of the cone.

Ladle melted paraffin onto the outside of the steel-grass-covered cone to create an icy effect.

Double rows of opaque milky white glass bottles form a versatile composite centerpiece for holiday entertaining, and filled with exquisite and exotic blossoms like Amazon lilies (*Eucharis*), turmeric (*Curcuma*), and stars-of-Bethlehem (*Ornithogalum*), they provide captivating, nontraditional floral fare. The water in the vases, which causes the containers to appear two toned, is at even levels in this design, but it could be varied for a different effect.

These flower-covered orbs are positioned atop steel-grass-covered, cone-shaped "pedestals." To create an ultra-hip complexion, the cones are coated with paraffin.

STEPHEN SMITH

STEPHEN SMITH

LEFT & OPPOSITE PAGE
To the English, gardening is not just a hobby; it's way of life. This Christmas display, influenced by the formally manicured plants and trees that typify English gardens, showcases topiary art, garden ornamentation, and nature's neutral color palette of whites and greens. Sort of a "nature-made-elegant" theme, that naturalism here is more controlled than wild—a tended garden as opposed to a wild thicket. Amidst a collection of texturally differing round forms, a silver ornament—reminiscent of a garden gazing ball—is nestled in a ring of preserved roses and foliage.

how-to
carnation snowball

Insert miniature carnation buds and blooms into a small (4 1/2") floral foam sphere so that each protrudes about 2 inches from the sphere.

Continue until the sphere is covered. Five or six bunches of miniature carnations are required, and the finished ball will be about 8 inches in diameter.

Encircle the ball with strands of silver bullion and lily grass (*Liriope*). Display the "snowball" in a decorative glass or aluminum dish.

OPPOSITE PAGE Bundled and placed diagonally into a narrow oval vase, stems of paperwhites (*Narcissus*) and lily grass (*Liriope*) make an artistic design statement. Resting atop the opening of the glass container and stabilizing the flowers are a pair of "frosty" glass bead ornaments. Showcasing the same elements, a smaller companion arrangement is designed into a glass bubble bowl, the inside of which is encircled with blades of lily grass.

STEPHEN SMITH

ABOVE Arranged in a floral foam sphere, long-lasting spray carnations, encircled by a "cage" of lily grass, form a contemporary floral object in the most popular of geometric forms. Nestled amidst branches of fir in a triangular bowl, this "snowball" becomes an artful and modern centerpiece.

STEPHEN SMITH

A check pattern is a dominant motif in this vignette as are round, square, and conical shapes. Subtle additions of green, from light to midrange, introduce an element of nature and temper the starkness of the black-and-white palette.

ABOVE Inspired by the allure of mid-20th-century Hollywood, this black, white, and silver themed square wreath comprises glamorous eclectic components such as feathers, sequins, jewels, and beads along with luxurious fabrics like velvet. The checkerboard mat/bulletin board is created from photocopies of post cards with cinematic images.

STEPHEN SMITH

Country Red

STEPHEN SMITH

OPPOSITE PAGE An exquisite blending of "woodland" botanicals, including pomegranate branches, Osage oranges (*Maclura*), bald cypress cones, smoke tree (*Cotinus*), privet, and pine, with vibrant red *Gerberas*, this texturally masterful arrangement beautifully conveys a casual country Christmas feeling.

how-to
standing wreath

Attach a coiled berried garland to a foam-filled urn with several greening pins.

ABOVE Although people traditionally place wreaths on walls or doors to express holiday sentiments, the round creations may also be used in freestanding designs or tabletop displays.

This quaint miniature wreath arrangement is fashioned atop an urn. Perhaps what is most interesting about it is its form. Instead of materials being arranged into a foam, vine, or poly wreath form, a coiled berried garland creates a round structure into which natural branches are woven. A cluster of permanent holly, pine cones, and pine cone rosettes adds a seasonal touch at the base.

how-to
stacked birds' nests

(see opposite page)

At the bottoms of three birds' nests, clip the wires that hold the nests together, and remove the bottoms of the nests.

Stack the nests together atop a foam-filled container, and insert stakes through the bundle into the foam. Add permanent pepperberries, and bind the bundle with permanent vines for more security.

Insert a vase into the center of the bundle of nests to hold a votive candle. Partially fill the vase with gravel to raise the votive candle to the desired height. Place a votive candle into the vase.

OPPOSITE PAGE Trios of twig birds' nests, with their bottoms removed, are stacked atop square wooden vases and around vases holding votive candles. Each bundle of nests is secured with wrappings of natural-looking permanent wired vines and permanent pepperberries. A pillar candle "garden" harmoniously completes the composition.

STEPHEN SMITH

ABOVE A simple design of berries, cones, and foliage is ideal for this uniquely customized basket—the real center of interest in this composition. Strips of ribbon, with the aid of spray adhesive, are glued to a peeled willow basket, followed by small pieces of cedar, salal leaves, and touches of gold leaf.

RIGHT & OPPOSITE PAGE Featuring a profusion of colorful berries, a ready-made wreath is a wonderful accent for this setting. A weathered-looking wash tub, which has a preserved wreath placed around the rim, is filled with pomegranates and *Hypericum* berries. Garland-wrapped aged clay pots are simple yet attractive seasonal additions.

ABOVE The European style of clustered materials casually dropped into wonderful containers has become a favorite of American consumers, too. And this design, created in floral foam, delivers that casual look with the addition of a bird's-nest-like collar of permanent river root and excelsior that encircles and extends the rim of the decorative pot. The design's comfortable size makes it an ideal hostess gift, desk decoration, or even party favor.

how-to
euro nest

After arranging florals, tuck clumps of excelsior around the pot rim. Wrap permanent river root around the perimeter, tucking it into the arrangement and securing it to itself and other materials.

RIGHT Candle arrangements are a mainstay for Christmas, but without enclosed flames, they can leave people feeling apprehensive. Burning tall pillar candles can cause half-melted looks, and hot wax can drip onto the floral materials, causing a serious fire hazard.

The design shown here offers a safe, refillable alternative to traditional hurricane designs. The floral construction is essentially the same, but by using hurricane or cylindrical vases, filled with decorative gravel, votive candles are elevated to a safe distance above the flammable flowers and foliages. This updated assembly also allows replacement of the votive candles easily, frequently, and inexpensively.

STEPHEN SMITH

STEPHEN SMITH

LEFT & OPPOSITE PAGE This 21st-century version of "countrified" Christmas comfortably blends casual and rustic with classic and contemporary. A touch of Victorian inspiration is exemplified by the three-tiered floral centerpiece, which is contrasted by the stark modern statement made by the vase of reddish reeds. Additional contrast is introduced with rustic and aged patinas along with new, shiny surfaces. And rather than the traditional complementary pairing of red and green, this palette embraces yellowed greens and orangy reds for an updated holiday scheme.

STEPHEN SMITH

STEPHEN SMITH

ABOVE An elegant ornament, placed simply atop a bundle of starflower stems inside a vase, creates a contemporary "nest"like composition.

how-to
bird's nest basket
(see opposite page)

Tightly wrap three half pieces of medium-gauge wire with brown stem wrap, which will blend well with the nest and basket and, therefore, be unnoticeable.

Attach the nest to the top of a basket with the taped wire. Bend each piece of wire into a hairpin shape. Insert each piece first through the side of a nest, then through the rim of the basket. Twist to secure.

Create a collar of berries and foliage between the base of the nest and the rim of the basket by cutting a permanent berried vine garland into pieces and hot-gluing the pieces to the outside of the nest.

RIGHT This centerpiece, an interpretation of the landscape of the Scottish Highlands, features bicolor 'Fashion' roses clustered alongside vibrant 'Flaming Parrot' tulips, both of which are nestled in a lush composition of evergreens, berries, mosses, branches, and pods. An antler cradles the bright blossoms and provides a defining finishing touch.

BELOW Most vase designs feature a flower or a bouquet of flowers in water, with a few foliage accents inside the vase. Here, an unexpected look is achieved by adhering the foliage to the outside of the vase and making it a main element of the design. This arrangement combines the traditional holiday colors of red and green in a most nontraditional way, using hemlock to cover the vase and pine as an embellishment around the tulips. Hemlock is a perfect choice for this technique because it is flat and flexible and, therefore, can adhere to a curved vase easily. Finishing the design are pine cones, which make a nice accent in lieu of ribbon.

how-to
hemlock vase

Spray adhesive onto the back sides of sprigs of hemlock, and press the greenery onto a glass vase in an overlapping fashion.

Inspired by high-country wilderness, this woodland composition also has a distinctive air of formality. Sprays of crimson berries fan out through the center, and assorted woodsy foliages, in variations of seasonal colors, complete the arrangement in a structured style. Branches of permanent plumosus fern form a "canopy" over the other materials, and an antler candelabrum and twig orbs harmoniously accessorize the arrangement.

OPPOSITE PAGE Rich in tradition, the small-checked, red-background plaid featured here inspires holiday arrangements of customary colors. The lavish creation, which is sizeable enough for applications from an entryway decoration to a Christmas buffet centerpiece, has as its foundation a tall wooden candle stand. Crowning the arrangement is a magnificent orb of 'Charlotte' roses, which is collared by a profusion of evergreens, ivy, and winterberry branches, and a lush garland of the same materials is swirled around the candle stand alternately with a red plaid fabric.

how-to
evergreen garland
(see opposite page)

Roll the desired length of wire netting into a tube-shaped form, and fasten it into shape with wire.

ABOVE The modern styling of red carnations and winterberries *(Ilex)* is traditional in color and flower type only. It is innovatively designed by lacing, or interweaving, the winterberry stems to create a framework into which the carnations are arranged. Cranberries floating atop the water add another beautiful dimension to the arrangement.

Cut evergreen tips, winterberries, rosehips, and other materials of choice into equal-sized pieces, and place them into piles, ready for assembly.

Insert the stem ends of the materials into the netting "tube," in one direction, starting at the bottom and working toward the top. The garland can be one sided or all sided.

RIGHT With the inspiration of an abandoned garden, this fashionable country styling of berries, branches, and evergreens is befitting of a rural Christmas. Coniferous Hinoki cypress and leafy *Skimmia* are expertly paired for textural interplay, and red winterberries and red-orange rosehips are combined for a blend of holiday color. Vinelike rose stems, laden with more hips, provide rhythm throughout the centerpiece. With materials generously arranged on both the inner and outer sides of the wreath form, the open space in the center is purposely minimized. Taper candles are easily replaced in this season-lasting design.

OPPOSITE PAGE Creating an exciting color harmony, flowers in overall orangy red hues are selected to harmonize with the prominent russet tones of the plaid. In a modern composite design, 'Fashion' roses are combined with red-orange *Gerberas*. Casting a nod to cranberry bogs, stems of bear grass and floating cranberries fill the vases, and bridging the arrangement trio is a thorny wild plum branch, which has cranberries impaled on its thorns to resemble a fruited branch.

Merry Magenta

A vertical band of red, fuchsia, and gold plaid wired ribbon adds holiday accent to a simple bud vase. The ribbon is knotted at the top, with just enough room for a few slender stems. Here, fresh *Gloriosa* lilies fill this space, accented by two sizes of sphere-shaped Christmas ornaments lightly glued to the ribbon.

RIGHT This opulent and abundant wreath features all kinds of dissimilar florals and accessories: shiny ornaments are paired with natural cones and pods, and clusters of fresh statice are combined with an assortment of permanents. Notice that the poinsettias are given a bit of sparkle with gold leaf.

STEPHEN SMITH

STEPHEN SMITH

LEFT Presenting a playful departure from traditional potted plant decorations, spirited #40-width ribbons are folded in half and tied around the rims of brightly painted clay pots. The ribbons are knotted twice, and the "tails" are given perky chevron cuts.

BELOW Sparkling silver reflects the beauty of the season on this pretty tree. A foam cone covered in dried *Hydrangea* blossoms rests atop a foam sphere, which is wrapped with silver bead garland and nestled into a silver bullet vase. Bright silver ball ornaments encircle the cone, and at the top, of course, is a lovely Christmas star.

ABOVE Vibrant color is the prominent feature of this holiday tree. A potpourri of permanent flowers and berries in bright hues covers a foam cone, which is placed atop an elegant silver urn. Silver bullion encases the flower-covered cone. The finishing touch is a pretty silver tussie mussie holder, inverted and placed on top of the structure.

Filled with compact arrangements of silver *Brunia*, on the right, and Chinese miniature carnations, on the left, two elegant loving cups are outfitted with "ropes" of *Casuarina*, a native Australian pinelike foliage, for a sophisticated European flair. The *Casuarina* is bound with thin silver beading wire, then wound around and tucked and wired into the arrangements. Accenting the designs is a pillar candle that is artfully placed atop a silver twig star, which is resting on the opening of an urn.

ABOVE European-style mouth-blown glass ornaments, in purple and red jewel tones and all different textures, give this PVC-based wreath a look that is almost regal. Beaded acrylic berries and miniature apples in a variety of glittering finishes accent the rich colors of the ornaments, as do clusters of velvety grape hyacinths and Victorian "hand-tied" posies with beaded detailing.

OPPOSITE PAGE Fashioned of glittering mouth-blown glass ornaments, beaded eggs, and small nosegays accented with miniature glass balls, this opulent creation, which is anything but traditional, features a "frame" of alternating orange and fuchsia ostrich drabs. Velvety holly leaves outlined with glitter provide a rich accent to the overall look of the PVC-based wreath and its trendy fuchsia and golden-copper color scheme.

how-to
advent wreath

Soak an 8.5-inch-diameter floral foam wreath form in flower-food solution. Insert four taper candles, evenly spaced, into the foam wreath.

Set the foam wreath atop a glass vase, and arrange *Hydrangea* blossoms into the foam. Make sure to cover all mechanics.

Arrange the remainder of the floral materials into the foam wreath, and weave pieces of steel grass through the flowers.

STEPHEN SMITH

Advent wreaths have been Christian symbols of the coming of Christ since the Middle Ages. Traditionally, they are composed of four candles in a circle of evergreens, but this wreath offers a contemporary take on classic advent wreaths through the addition of color, texture, and a stylish look. Like the traditional symbol, it showcases three purple candles and one rose candle, but flowers in coordinating hues add a nontraditional flair. Steel grass is crisscrossed throughout the design in a contemporary manner, and a bold purple vase elevates the composition.

Because this design includes fresh flowers, which do not last as long as traditional evergreen foliages, it is ideal for the final week of Advent or for a Christmas Eve celebration—the final day the candles are traditionally lit.

A nontraditional, nearly complementary color combination imparts a modern and almost Southern vibrancy to this elegant designer-made tree. The composition of materials, somewhat more traditional for the holidays, includes satin-finish glass ornaments, miniature Czechoslovakian fruits, and millinery-quality permanent flowers along with a glorious preserved butterfly. Cleverly, a silver tussie-mussie holder, when inverted, becomes a distinctive finial-like tree topper.

LEFT Topiaries in Christmas tree form appear to be covered with candied fruits while mercury glass balls and a glittery Santa brighten the muted pastels.

OPPOSITE PAGE Sugar-coated fruits arranged on a silver tiered epergne are accented with shiny ornaments and mercury glass balls. Placed on a mirrored plateau, this fruitful display is especially appropriate for holiday entertaining.

LEFT With a foam form as a base, this natural, highly textural wreath is created with a variety of fresh, permanent, preserved, and dried florals. Fresh *Eucalyptus* and statice, which will air dry in place, are combined with permanent ivy, preserved *Hydrangeas*, and dried reindeer moss. Silver Victorian posy holders, filled with miniature bouquets of similar materials, and glass ornaments add sparkle and create a pleasing contrast.

OPPOSITE PAGE Cool hues of blue and violet combine with shimmery silver to make this permanent, conical topiary the perfect winter decorative, regardless of the holiday. By stacking blocks of floral foam, first horizontally, then vertically; stabilizing them with dowels; and trimming the top brick to shape, an inexpensive cone-shaped form is created. In addition to the dried materials, the topiary features permanent *Delphinium* blossoms and silver-painted foliage along with a variety of ornaments including those with the look of trendy mercury glass. A sheer, wired-edge ribbon adds a festive rhythm to the design

how-to
heather dove

ABOVE & OPPOSITE PAGE Lovely tints and shades of red and red-violet combine with white to create an exquisite plaid, which is the inspiration for this captivating holiday composition. Floral materials, including rich magenta-colored thistles similar to those portrayed on the Scottish royal emblem, and heather, which is native to Scotland, are chosen for their heritage as well as their color coordination with the plaid.

In the spectacular design, which would be exquisite on a holiday buffet, a dove, fashioned of fresh heather, alights amid thistles and evergreens arranged atop a bronze candlestick. Dramatically cascading from the composition, a thistle-filled hunting horn, also made of heather, extends the arrangement to the tabletop.

Create a round head and a teardrop-shaped body out of dry flower foam. Cover with bits of heather by wrapping with paddle wire. Insert long stems of heather into the narrow end of the body to create the tail.

Insert long stems of heather into both sides of the body to make the wings. Wrap the stems of heather with paddle wire and shape each wing into desired formations.

Attach the round head to the body with a wood pick and hot glue. To make a beak, cut one end of a small piece of branch on an angle, and hot-glue the blunt end into the head.

how-to
heather-covered bowl

Lay two or three pieces of wire parallel to each other. Place stems of heather on top of and perpendicular to the wires. Wrap each wire once around each piece of heather until a "fence"like structure is made.

Place the heather structure around the container to be covered. A slightly flared container is the best choice. Securely tie the two ends together so that the structure is tight against the container.

Construct a heather "garland" to the length of the circumference of the container's base. Wrap the "garland" around the base, and secure the ends together. This will camouflage the ends of the heather stems.

OPPOSITE PAGE Fragrant flat cedar and a mix of bicolor carnations, including 'Bright Rendevous,' 'Cinderella,' and 'Fagiano,' are elegantly showcased in a silver-plated Victorian epergne, which displays four tussie-mussie holders on two tiers. The elevated, multilevel design makes a grand holiday presentation. The interplay of color within each of the bicolor blossoms—as well as among the different varieties—adds to the drama of this striking piece.

STEPHEN SMITH

ABOVE A mounded centerpiece of pink peonies and hyacinths, arranged with scarlet 'Charlotte' roses and magenta thistle blossoms, is designed in a custom-crafted, heather-covered container.

Bright roses open summertime possibilities for this wreath, which radiates a distinct English garden feeling. However, berry sprays, permanent evergreens, and dried dusty miller accents help to also make it a perfect choice for Christmas. The materials are set into a foam wreath form with picks and hot glue.

RIGHT Elegant, two-tiered arrangements are perhaps the most desirable and impacting centerpieces for creating festive holiday tables, and an affordable epergnelike container can be constructed easily by hot-gluing a tall, wide-neck bud vase to the top of a piece of floral foam in a round plastic tray. Then, a foam cage is hot-glued atop the vase, and the fresh florals are arranged into the cage. Because wax cannot be hot-glued to floral foam, the ball candle is attached to a piece of duct tape, which is, in turn, glued to the foam.

STEPHEN SMITH

STEPHEN SMITH

LEFT Although the appearance is that the vibrantly colored flowers are arranged into this shapely sweet-heart vase, the truth is that they are arranged into a foam cage, which is glued to the top of the vase. The ball candle is secured to the foam cage prior to the flowers' insertion.

RIGHT & OPPOSITE PAGE
Chosen to display the
Czechoslovakian ornaments,
this line of silver urns offers
several exquisite styles and
sizes. In the background,
opulent topiaries of
permanent florals and
seashell ornaments are
stunning tabletop designs
that accent the décor.

Spicy Orange

Influenced by heirloom linens and bed coverings, these florals are chosen to evoke an English garden, and they're of soft colors as well, such as the pristine lilies-of-the-valley and apricot/peach 'Versilia' roses. The Victorian-flavor arrangement is designed atop an antique iron candlestick.

STEPHEN SMITH

STEPHEN SMITH

LEFT Varying levels of light add interest to a versatile display of tan-and-ivory pots. The pots contain both tapers and ball candles, each surrounded by fuchsia-tipped cream-colored carnations and red sweetheart roses with *Ruscus* foliage.

RIGHT Three two-tone, banded pillar candles are nestled inside three identically-sized urns. The urns have weathered appearances that work well with the colors of their contents. *Coleus* foliage picks up the caramel color of each candle's band, and feather plumes are interspersed among two colors of carnations—one that is a parchment yellow and one that is parchment yellow with a red variegation.

STEPHEN SMITH

RIGHT Although laden with the traditional colors of Christmas, this tree has a distinct Far East flavor. The tree topper, a pagoda-like garden torch that holds a votive candle, has been threaded through the tree.

OPPOSITE PAGE Saturated floral foam rings are arranged with *Galax* leaves, red-tipped huckleberry, *Hypericum* berries, and two varieties of carnations—'Sunset' and 'Eruption'—to resemble small fresh wreaths. The "wreaths," laid atop pedestal candleholders, become candle rings, encircling burgundy pillar candles. The composition's color range, from brown to burgundy to orange, is accented by hints of yellow found within the bicolor carnations, all of which coordinate for a fabulous traditionally styled yuletide presentation.

OPPOSITE PAGE Beautiful ribbons and bows are common finishing touches to holiday packages, but there is nothing common about this exquisite ruffled topper. Fashioned of #100-width wire-edged dupioni silk ribbon, it is highlighted with metallic gold leaves and an ornate gold bead in the center.

In a bow-making manner, gather a 2- to 3-foot length of #100-width wired ribbon, only gather the ribbon down the center rather than from side to side.

Tie off the gathered ribbon with a wire, and shape it into a ruffly-edged "rosette."

STEPHEN SMITH

Hot-glue a gold-headed boutonniere pin into the center of a decorative bead, and pin the bead to the box through the center of the rosette. Finish by hot-gluing in a few leaves.

ABOVE Expressive of the last vestiges of a fall garden and the onset of winter, a densely arranged assortment of permanent materials is at home among "ice"-encrusted branches of a permanent pine wreath. Imparting the dried, end-of-season garden ambience are permanent rosehips and cranberry branches, seed pods of *Clematises* and poppies, and chestnuts. Dried *Protea* flowers and assorted cones complete this exquisite yet subtle seasonal composition.

117

how-to
fruit votives

Trace the bottom diameter of a votive candle onto a piece of fruit. Carve out a section of fruit deep enough to accommodate the entire votive candle.

Cover the base of the votive candle with plastic wrap to prevent the wick from absorbing moisture from the fruit. Insert the votive into the hole in the fruit.

Insert a wooden pick into the bottom of each piece of fruit, and arrange the fruit into a container filled with white pine and incense cedar.

OPPOSITE PAGE A texturally wondrous "tapestry" arrangement captures a Native American spirit. The 'Orange Unique' roses reflect sunsets, and the color and texture of the reversed *Magnolia* leaves echo tanned deer skin. On the floor, a rustic basket is filled with real birds' nests and shed feathers from hawks, turkeys, and other wild fowl.

STEPHEN SMITH

ABOVE Positioned atop a lush bed of incense cedar, flat cedar, and pine boughs, which have been arranged lavishly into a floral-foam-filled bowl, a collection of fresh citrus fruits becomes deliciously fragrant candleholders. The oranges, lemons, and limes are hollowed out with a knife, and candles, in hues corresponding with the respective fruits, are placed inside.

A stunning vase arrangement of peach- and rose-colored florals beautifies a formal dining room that, swathed in creamy ivory hues with peach- and wine-colored accents, has a Victorian ambience.

STEPHEN SMITH

LEFT Covered with four rich patterns of ribbon, this "tree" has an opulent yet contemporary styling. A random wrapping of gold beading wire provides a garland effect, and gold, pearl-headed corsage pins become the ornaments. An inverted tussie-mussie holder is positioned atop the tree and camouflages the mechanics.

how-to
fabric tannenbaum

Pin lengths of ribbon vertically to a plastic foam cone with straight pins beginning at the top where the ribbon is curled (tubelike) to the bottom where it is uncurled.

Wrap the ribbon-covered cone randomly with gold beading wire, and insert clusters of pearl-head corsage pins as ornaments. Hot-glue the cone onto an urn.

Hot-glue a tussie-mussie holder on top of the ribbon-covered cone as a decorative tree topper and to hide the mechanics.

OPPOSITE PAGE Atop an ornately filigreed silver pedestal swagged with garlanded beads, preserved and permanent florals are combined with beaded fruits and berries. Colorful antique glass ornaments are ideal accessories as is the hand-painted Slavic Santa recreated from an antique ice-cream mold.

STEPHEN SMITH

ABOVE Displaying bits of candied fruits, garden cloches provide mouth-watering tabletop accents.

LEFT In accordance with European tradition, a Victorian Christmas tree is dressed with sugarplums, sweetmeats, and small bouquets of flowers. Our modern-day version features glistening glass balls and fruit ornaments, iced fruit pomanders, and silver cones filled with small clusters of permanent rose blossoms.

STEPHEN SMITH

A beautiful and fragrant edging of Christmas greens, including pine, fir, and hemlock, transforms a vibrant collection of bicolor carnations into a gorgeous seasonal centerpiece. Strategic foliage placements enhance the carnations and allow them, with all their wonderful color and texture patterns, to take center stage and to truly shine bright this holiday season.

STEPHEN SMITH

STEPHEN SMITH

Cut off the bottom one-third of *Kunzea* stems, and arrange them vertically and tightly clustered into the center of the container. This provides support for the longer pieces, which are arranged next.

Arrange the remaining upper two-thirds portions of the *Kunzea* stems vertically around the tightly massed center cluster of stems.

With a touch of holiday whimsy, this Dr. Seuss-influenced tree design is fashioned from long stems of *Kunzea* foliage, a myrtle family relative with leaves that are pungently aromatic when crushed. The "jewels" encircling the tree (pieces of disassembled ornaments like the one that hangs from the drooping tip of the tree) are attached to length of beading wire and wrapped around the bound *Kunzea* foliage.

Bind the arranged stems with beading wire, from the bottom to the top, to form the tapered shape. Then, make a garland of ornaments with more beading wire, and wrap it around the "tree."

Contemporary Red

Not commonly perceived as Christmas blossoms in most of the country, exotic red *Anthuriums* can add a dash of excitement to holiday décor. Here, arranged with a topiary influence, permanent versions of the tropical flowers are accented with an eclectic assortment of more traditional holiday ornaments.

STEPHEN SMITH

Punch holes in the centers of small *Magnolia* leaves with a paper punch. Spray some of the leaves with gold paint.

Slide the leaves, in a random color pattern, onto the *Gerbera* stem and up to the bloom. Rotate the leaves to form a petal-like effect.

Tie a shoelace-type bow of braided cord, and attach it to the flower stem, just beneath the leaves, with a corsage pin.

In an enchanting twist on a single-flower bud vase, a rich velvety red *Gerbera* daisy is transformed into a striking holiday "composite flower" with a multilayer, petal-like collar of fresh green and gold *Magnolia* leaves. Cut short and placed just atop the opening of a contemporary art-glass vase, this floral creation, which has a multitude of holiday applications including a nosegay to carry, also features a simple, updated bowlike treatment of braided cord.

RIGHT With the help of a classic bulb-bottom bud vase, the elongated neck of which is wrapped with red and gold cording, eight roses and a ball candle form a quick yet clever arrangement which has a variety of holiday entertaining applications.

BELOW When wrapped around glass candlesticks, vases, pots, and the like, strands of beads create original "jewel"-encrusted containers.

STEPHEN SMITH

STEPHEN SMITH

OPPOSITE PAGE A new twist on traditional ribbon-wrapped wreaths, this handicraft creation features an assortment of seven ribbons in widths from 1/4 inch to 2 1/2 inches, some of which are folded in half. Each piece of ribbon is cut and tied on individually, wraps around the wreath only once, and is knotted at the outside edge of the wreath. All of the "tails" are cut to equal lengths, giving the wreath a fluffy, feathery edge, and profuse overlapping of the ribbons gives the wreath its distinctive appearance. The metallic gold feather ribbon is tied on last at random intervals.

Holiday classics, plaids create a Christmas ambience in a traditional manner, and collections of ornaments displayed in bowls add to that ambience in a modern manner. Orb-shaped floral designs, like this lush ball of preserved roses, capitalize on the popularity of spheres as decorative elements and bring the trend into the botanical realm.

Christmas ornaments double as bud vases with just a few simple steps and materials. Shiny red mercury glass balls are set inside pots and "belted" with permanent curly vine. The tops of the glass balls are removed, leaving holes just large enough to hold single stems of permanent *Ranunculi*.

how-to
ornamental vases

Using a paint brush, apply hot glue around the inside rim of a pot, and place a mercury glass ball into the pot.

RIGHT Although the geometric form of these miniature ornament-covered "trees" and the urns upon which they sit are traditional classics, these ready-made decoratives have a contemporary flair that gives them an eclectic character and versatility.

OPPOSITE PAGE Secured atop the rim of a square metal container, a permanent evergreen wreath is reshaped to fit, and a rich collection of ornaments and botanicals is hot-glued among the branches. Exquisitely detailed ornaments, resting atop crumpled butcher paper that fills the container, complete the design. An accessory piece features a square dried *Hydrangea* "wreath" laid atop a low square metal vessel.

STEPHEN SMITH

Varying shades of red create excitement in a component design of *Gerberas*. Each stem is arranged into a contemporary organic bud vase partially filled with red craft gravel. Shiny Christmas ornaments, also in shades of red, accentuate the arrangement and, when placed tightly together with the bud vases, cause a delightful reflection. Floral tints provide the option of slightly altering the color of flowers, and tinting the water is another option for increasing visual impact.

STEPHEN SMITH

These cylinder vases show two ways of using ribbon to accent water-filled designs. Simple waterproof, shimmering red ribbons are used inside a vase of water to surround ornaments and a bunch of *Trachelium*, and they are also used outside another vase to give ornaments a new perspective. Try using a small dab of clear superglue to attach the ornaments to the dry cylinders. When water is added, this will keep them immersed rather than floating to the top.

OPPOSITE PAGE Oversized bubble-ball votive holders, which have open bottoms, are filled with glittered branches and shiny translucent berries. Expanding the theme are a luscious red raspberry wreath and a glass bowl filled with glittered fruit.

RIGHT The 5-inch opening on this pedestal vase makes the container ideal for both tapers and flowers. A bundle of six 24-inch-tall tapers is taped together at the base and dropped into the vase. Resting at the bottom of the 10-inch-tall vase, the bundle of tapers is kept upright by the fresh florals which are wedged between the candles and the sides of the vase.

STEPHEN SMITH

OPPOSITE PAGE Beautiful as floral containers, gift boxes, or even holiday decoratives, these opulent accessories are easily created by wrapping gold-painted chipwood boxes with a luxurious #100-width, wire-edged, velvet ribbon. The lid is also adorned with a square piece of the ribbon as well as a glittery gold leaf. All materials can be affixed with spray adhesive or hot glue.

STEPHEN SMITH

ABOVE Red, cream-colored, and candy-striped carnation balls are created on floral foam spheres for simple tabletop decorations. The solid colors allow the carnation balls to coordinate perfectly with solid red, white, and cream-colored ball candles. These designs make delightful accents for parties. If they are to be used on linens, however, placing glass plates underneath is a good idea to contain seepage from the floral foam.

Multiple levels of flowers and light lend a contemporary architectural approach to a centerpiece design. The geometric component arrangement comprises various sized square wooden boxes, lined and filled with soaked floral foam, with carnations arranged inside so that the flower heads are flush with the rims of the boxes. The lids of the boxes contain carnation petals, and square candles in two natural shades repeat the shapes of the boxes and lids throughout the design. This design is especially versatile because the boxes may be displayed upright, on their sides, or in a combination of both positions.

To create this simple yet striking holiday decorative, a multiwick wax cube is placed into the center of a larger wax box. Floating in the space between the cube and the box, which is filled with water, are red standard carnations that frame the candle. The blossoms can be refreshed throughout the holiday season.

The vertically parallel arrangement of permanent
amaryllises, which rise above a "hedge" of permanent
evergreens, reflects both the newness and naturalness
that is central to this contemporary red look.

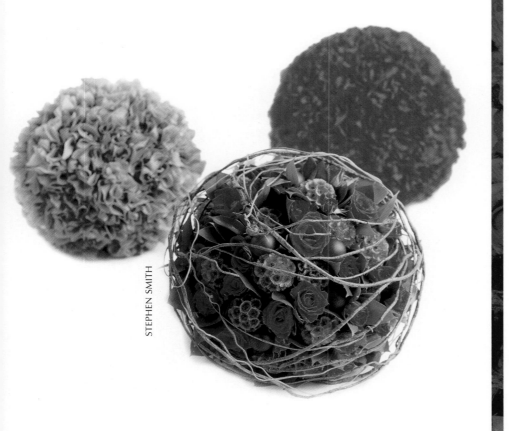

Floral spheres began showing up several years ago, and their popularity seems to be gaining—long after one might have expected them to loose their faddish charm.

The popularity of geometric forms in design could have something to do with it. Simple shapes are definitely part of pop culture. The American fascination with gardening, which includes manicured geometric shapes in the art of topiary, strengthens the appeal.

how-to
parallel amaryllises
(see opposite page)

Hot-glue dry foam into the center of a rectangular container, leaving a 1-inch space between the foam and all sides of the container.

Arrange permanent foliage vertically between the foam and container edges to create a hedgelike appearance. Arrange smaller pieces vertically into the foam to cover the top of the foam.

Insert two 6-inch wood picks opposite each other into the sides of a permanent amaryllis stem. Wrap wire around the base of the stem and the picks to secure the picks to the stem and keep them parallel.

RIGHT Rather than hanging on a wall or door, these ready-made berry wreaths are "planted" in terra cotta clay pots to form delightful topiaries, which can be placed around the home as mix-and-match holiday accessories.

LEFT Ready-made items such as the wild pine wreath, berry spheres, and cranberry topiary can be quickly enhanced with ribbon or placed into pots for easy yet enticing holiday wares. A ready-made millet berry arrangement needs no additional adornment.

146

Displaying the most traditional colors of the Christmas season—deep burgundy red, crisp green, and snow white—these coordinating pieces, composed in three ceramic pots in differing sizes, capture the breathtaking beauty of the holiday season. Essential to the presentation are the red-banded pillar candles, each of which is adorned at its base with a band of either burgundy-red carnations or fragrant incense cedar. And in the background, a sumptuous mound of carnations is accented by a wrapping of incense cedar.

A striking and innovative interpretation of the wreath form, this vibrant, contemporary design features a modern glass bowl encircled by frosted glass votive candleholders. The bowl is filled with fresh cranberries that function as the arranging medium for the rich velvety red flowers—'Red Jewel' roses, amaryllises, *Ranunculi*, and *Gerberas*. More cranberries and *Ranunculi* fill the candleholders, and chopped blades of steel grass are placed casually around the votives to impart an Asian ambience and complete the traditional Christmas color harmony.

STEPHEN SMITH

LEFT Tradition has it that ivy symbolizes prosperity and charity. How appropriate, then, that ivy is also associated with Christmas, a time of year when the rewards of life are celebrated and the less fortunate are remembered. Particularly in England, ivy is as much a symbol of Christmas as holly and mistletoe, where it is a reminder to be thankful for all the gifts of life and an encouragement to joyfully share blessings with others. With that in mind, this delightful ivy creation will inspire reverent holiday celebration. The 14-inch-diameter potted ivy wreath is lined with a ready-made raspberry wreath that is wired into the center.

RIGHT A beautiful collectible, this ruby red glass ornament is multifunctional; designed to hold water, it allows for the presentation of fresh flowers on Christmas trees.

STEPHEN SMITH

how-to
magnolia-edged wreath
(see opposite page)

Glue *Magnolia* leaves, reverse side out, to the edge of a floral foam wreath with spray adhesive. Add two more layers of leaves in an overlapping "shingle-style" manner.

With sharp shears, cut the bottoms of the leaves flush with the bottom of the wreath.

Arrange several varieties of red roses into the floral foam wreath in two rings and at the same height.

STEPHEN SMITH

Ruby red glassware is a natural for the season, and these dramatic carafe-shaped vases, with copper wire wrappings and sentiment tags, extend holiday wishes in a decidedly modern manner.

150

Built up along its inner and outer edges with three layers of fresh *Magnolia* leaves, this contemporary table wreath appears to be designed in a gelatin mold-type container, but is actually dispersed into a floral foam wreath form. For an unusual color presentation, the tobacco-colored reverse sides of the *Magnolia* leaves are positioned outward. And to achieve a dimension of color unachievable with only one or two varieties of roses, 10 cultivars of red roses, ranging from pinkish red to crimson to deep burgundy, are combined. They are arranged around the wreath in two rings and at the same height.

RIGHT & OPPOSITE PAGE Entirely composed of the fruits of various botanicals, this lush wreath exudes Christmas spirit with modern yet traditional style. The red berried materials include *Skimmia* and rosehips, and the green berrylike botanicals are chinaberries (*Melia*), seeded *Eucalyptus*, and tiny Western hemlock (*Tsuga*) cones. This grand creation can be accessorized to achieve moods from casual to formal, the latter of which is accomplished with 16 silver votive candles. Throughout the season, this centerpiece should retain its beauty as the materials evolve from fresh to dried.

LEFT Exhibiting an industrial influence, this pair of cascading mound designs can imbue a holiday warmth to even the most starkly contemporary interiors. The compositions of permanent *Hydrangeas*, dried cockscomb, and berried vines are handsomely accented with metal bowls showcasing spheres of red permanent roses.

how-to
tower of flowers

Cut a block of wet floral foam into a cylindrical shape with a knife.

Insert sturdy branches into one end of the foam, stilt-like, to raise the foam out of the vase.

Place the branch-supported block of foam into a glass cylinder vase so that the bottom 2 or 3 inches of the foam are in the vase.

OPPOSITE PAGE Arranged into a floral foam sphere in a stone bowl, Christmassy red carnations are accented with a "belt" of permanent vines. The spherical form is repeated with round filigree ornaments in a matching bowl, which provides unity to the setting.

STEPHEN SMITH

ABOVE Inspired by the topiary form, this modern design comprises red carnations and the off-white berries and two-tone foliage of *Cotoneaster*. Placed vertically inside the glass vase are pieces of thick curly willow branches, which support a block of wet floral foam positioned on end, atop the branches, to rise out of the vase. Concealing the portion of the block of foam that is inside the vase are sprigs of Aussie pine (*Calothamnus*). Ideal for a holiday party, this design's longevity will be somewhat shorter than normal because, although the floral materials are arranged in the wet foam, their stems don't reach down in the water.

ABOVE & OPPOSITE PAGE Fusing contemporary, geometric forms with classic elements, this heterogenous assemblage of floral materials exudes a European spirit that is clean and ordered yet comfortable. The contrast of crisp red and white, with traditional holiday green omitted, along with the blending of sumptuousness and handicraft, creates additional "tension," giving these most traditional holiday colors a thoroughly modern look.

Woodland Hues

STEPHEN SMITH

OPPOSITE PAGE With its precise balance of smooth and coarse textures, this masculine, monochromatic styling offers maximum visual interest. The materials—striped squash, miniature gourds, bell cups, natraj, *Canella* berries, and mahogany pods—although decidedly autumnal, can easily make the transition from fall holidays to Christmas celebrations with the addition of metallic ornaments, perhaps in a mix of shiny and matte finishes.

LEFT A pickled wood jardiniere makes a stylish stand for this narrow tree decorated with ornaments in neutral hues. The natural decorations, which include pine cones, assorted dried pods, bleached ostrich feathers, and more, are enhanced by shimmering bows tied from gold and silver ribbon.

how-to
fresh candle ring
(see opposite page)

Drill three narrow holes into the bottom of a pillar candle. Insert wooden picks into the holes.

Place the candle on top of a piece of saturated floral foam in a ceramic pot, with the wooden picks going into the floral foam.

Arrange *Hypericum*, pine cones, nuts, and foliage into the foam around the candle. Arrange permanent vines to swirl over the top of the floral materials.

OPPOSITE PAGE Coffee-scented candles are the inspiration for this collection of texture-rich holiday decoratives. The centerpiece, in a cappuccino-colored pot, features an energizing blend of fresh pine, pine cones, *Hypericum* berries, and walnuts around an Espresso banded candle. Permanent vines and a disassembled miniature honeysuckle vine wreath top off the design. Additional Espresso candles, placed on aromatic fresh beans in more cappuccino-hued pots or their coordinating trays, are tasteful accents.

ABOVE Today's woodland look is sophisticated and clean, and it has a natural yet magical appearance, as depicted by the golden eggs.

STEPHEN SMITH

OPPOSITE PAGE The design technique of grouping reinforces the volume of this wreath embellished with pine cones, seed pods, and a variety of other dried materials, all on wood picks. The materials are constructed on a foam wreath form. This transseasonal wreath would be ideal in a country atmosphere but would also be beautiful in a sophisticated, neoclassic setting for contrast.

STEPHEN SMITH

BELOW In a modern mosaic vase, an iced snowball ornament is surrounded by antique-colored fabric roses in an interesting juxtaposition of hues: fresh snow against warm caramels and creams.

STEPHEN SMITH

ABOVE This wreath comprises natural Southern elements and makes a charming addition to any garden-inspired room. Materials include realistic-looking permanent *Echevarias*, wispy Oriental pines, other permanent evergreens, and Spanish moss, with a few berried clusters intermixed.

RIGHT Old-world collectible Santas, traditional Christmas favorites, find their place within this rustic gathering, where an old-fashioned bread bowl filled with river rocks serves as a candleholder for a trio of pillar candles.

STEPHEN SMITH

STEPHEN SMITH

OPPOSITE PAGE Rusted iron urns are the perfect containers for these earth-toned foliage arrangements, which include seeded balls and pewter-colored pine cones. A tin Moravian star, actually a votive candleholder, fits comfortably in this setting, as do the bird's nest and old-fashioned bread bowls.

OPPOSITE PAGE   Although it prominently adorns a ladder-back chair, this lush permanent swag of fruit, foliage, feathers, and natural orb ornaments is created on one half of a plastic foam wreath form, making it easy to hang anywhere in the home. Burlap ribbon enhances the textural, woodsy feeling.

ABOVE   This hand-carved Nativity is just what one might expect to find adorning a ranch home on the Ponderosa. Inspired by sun-dried timberland materials that are spiced with touches of bittersweet orange, the ever-popular natural Christmas look is updated with a Southwestern aesthetic for weathered surfaces and simple rough-hewn accessories.

how-to
band of pine cones
(see opposite page)

Arrange a mass of preserved noble fir into a flared container.

Attach wired wood picks to the tips of several piñon pine cones.

Hot-glue the wood-picked pine cones into the mass of greenery in a row through the center of the arrangement.

STEPHEN SMITH

ABOVE & OPPOSITE PAGE A perennial favorite, today's woodland look has gone to finishing school. It's more sophisticated and "cleaned up," with the influence of classic architectural elements and geometric forms. It can also be described as modern flea-market chic. Design is simple yet structured, casual yet formal. Indicative of the look are a four-branch candelabrum with simple nestlike arrangements (opposite page) and a square "wreath" (above), which is heavily encrusted with natural woodsy elements.

OPPOSITE PAGE   A bounteous collection of cones, assorted pods, and sponge mushrooms is glued into a PVC wreath, giving these traditional autumn elements an opportunity to decorate homes for fall and also herald the winter season. The PVC wreath is secured to a bamboo plate, so instead of an empty center, this grand composition appears to be laid upon a freshly cut tree.

STEPHEN SMITH

ABOVE   A mixture of cones and pods, which provides a wonderful array of colors and textures, is arranged to allow some of the permanent evergreen wreath to remain visible. The materials, including laranja (*Mauritia*) and thika (*Raphia*) pods, belani apples, and several genera of cones, are arranged in all positions, from upright to sideways to upside down, for greater interest. Branches of permanent wired curly willow impart rhythm into the design.

STEPHEN SMITH

ABOVE   Creating a rustic lushness, two genera of miniature cones, gum nuts (*Eucalyptus*), and gray and chartreuse lichens densely cover a medium-sized permanent evergreen wreath. The evergreen branchlets are bent in half to make a tighter, well-groomed base.

RIGHT The square shape of this "wreath" adds an element of surprise and excitement. Dried cones and pods, moss, and preserved foliage are hot-glued to the contemporary shape, the base of which is a square foam form. This distinctive wreath is a great addition to both contemporary and country settings year-round.

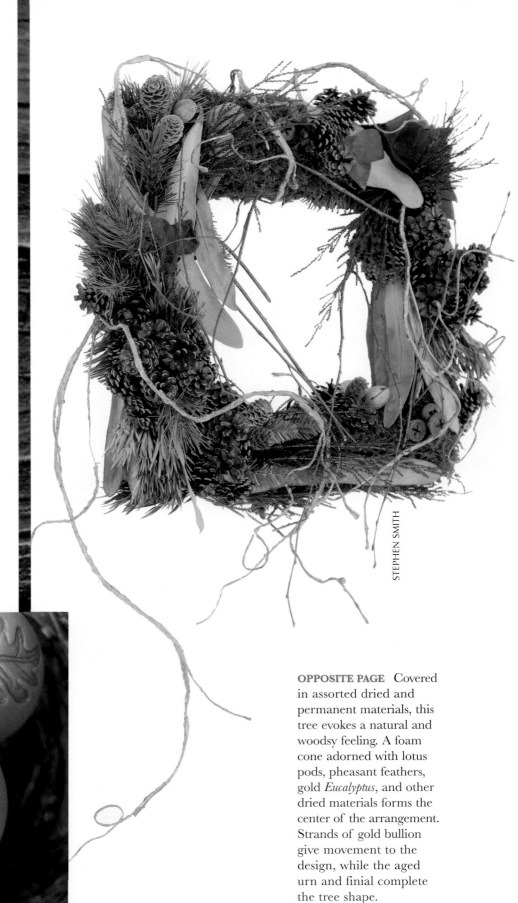

OPPOSITE PAGE Covered in assorted dried and permanent materials, this tree evokes a natural and woodsy feeling. A foam cone adorned with lotus pods, pheasant feathers, gold *Eucalyptus*, and other dried materials forms the center of the arrangement. Strands of gold bullion give movement to the design, while the aged urn and finial complete the tree shape.

Christmas Blue

STEPHEN SMITH

OPPOSITE PAGE Beautifully accessorized with silver, blue has a place at the Christmas table, as is demonstrated with this simplistic setting of blue candles and Christmas ornaments, some of which are tucked into a boxwood centerpiece arranged into a silver compote.

ABOVE A blueberry wreath and an arrangement of dried lavender are fashionable ready-made accents while gothic pillar candles, in silver Revere bowls, are seasonally enhanced with boxwood, multihued berries, and tiny glass ornaments.

OPPOSITE PAGE Offering a distinctive color harmony for the holidays, this arrangement features oversized handmade "ornaments" in a large-checked, blue-based plaid. A Scottish Highlands theme is carried through with magenta-colored thistles (*Cirsium*), heatherlike *Thryptomene*, and incense cedar.

RIGHT Elements in vibrant chartreuse hues, including small glass balls in shiny and matte finishes, add a "punch" to the analogous color harmony of this design and accentuate the narrow stripes of yellow that run through the blue plaid pattern. Additionally, the arrangement is a hand-tied bouquet that is held in position by the ball ornaments.

STEPHEN SMITH

A simple collection of natural woodland finds, including pine cones, fresh berried juniper, and a bird's nest with "robin eggs," takes on a wonderful icy ambience when "frozen" in place with paraffin. The materials are casually but artfully arranged into a bamboo bowl, which is coated with melted paraffin, and "frozen" in an "ice-covered pond" created with more paraffin. A drizzle of wax over the items completes the wintry scene.

STEPHEN SMITH

STEPHEN SMITH

For those who prefer nontraditional holiday decoratives, or for those who have homes and offices in which traditional Christmas colors don't work, this exquisite topiary, comprising both permanent and fresh floral materials, could be a lovely alternative. Constructed on rectangular blocks of floral foam and topped with an aged finial, this composition features permanent frosty ivy leaves and other faux botanicals, in subdued silver and blue-green hues, combined fresh white roses, for which fabric or freeze-dried blooms could be substituted.

how-to
icy bowl scene
(see opposite page)

Ladle melted paraffin into a bowl-shaped container, and roll the bowl in your hands to distribute the paraffin to the edges. Let cool, and repeat until desired whiteness is achieved.

Arrange pine cones, fresh juniper, and a bird's nest containing wooden eggs into the bowl in a natural manner.

Drizzle melted paraffin over the materials to secure them in place and to create a frozen, iced-over appearance.

how-to

silver pot vases

(see opposite page)

Spray a small clay pot and wooden candleholder with silver paint.

Hot-glue the small clay pot onto the inverted candle holder.

Glue satin cording and a silver button around the area where the pot and candle holder meet.

STEPHEN SMITH

For a stylish wall piece or welcoming door decoration, a root wreath is embellished with boxwood in shades of both light and dark green. Multihued berries and piñon pine cones are added to finish the design.

Featured in crackle-finish planter boxes, preserved blue *Hydrangeas* coordinate nicely with blue and chartreuse berries. Blue glass ornaments, in silver-painted, customized urns, make affordable accents.

STEPHEN SMITH

LEFT & OPPOSITE A total departure from traditional holiday color palettes, ocean-inspired hues, from blackened blues to blue-greens to yellow-greens, form the basis of these Christmas designs. Eclecticism is introduced with contrasting textures, which range from reflective to matte, along with ornamentation, the inspiration of which ranges from 19th-century Fabergé jeweling to 1960s Pucci pattern. In addition, the classicism of "estate" silver is juxtaposed with the modernness of shiny, colorful glass.

how-to
wax-covered bowl
(see opposite page)

Roll the bottom two-thirds or so of a glass bubble bowl in melted paraffin. Let cool, and repeat. The top edges of the paraffin should be irregular and wavy.

Pour melted paraffin inside the bowl, and roll the bowl, so that the paraffin coats all but the top one-third of the inside of the bowl. The top edges of the paraffin inside the bowl should be irregular and wavy.

Pour a small amount of melted paraffin into the bottom of the bowl, and immediately place a candle into the bowl. Wrap decorative monofilament around the outside of the bowl for a decorative effect.

STEPHEN SMITH

BELOW Clad in nontraditional Christmas colors, this spritely Santa, together with a white, pine-cone-shaped candle and shimmer wreath, embodies the contemporary spirit of the season. Fresh blue *Delphiniums* are the perfect floral accessory.

STEPHEN SMITH

STEPHEN SMITH

Representing the yin and yang of earthly elements—fire and ice—this custom-crafted candleholder, in arctic blue and white, is a clear glass bubble bowl that is partially "frosted," inside and out, with melted paraffin, then banded with decorative monofilament. The wavy edges of the wax coatings, which are varying thicknesses, randomly cross and overlap inside and outside the container. The wax treatment provides a captivating multidimensional opaque effect, especially when illuminated from within by the blue-and-white banded pillar candle, which is "ice bound" in a pool of wax in the bottom of the bubble bowl.

OPPOSITE PAGE These delicately fragrant lilies-of-the-valley have a subtle presence in this composition. The blue-and-white porcelain bowl is just one piece in the blended collection of Delftware-like platters, plates, and bowls, which feature pastoral scenes and floral patterns.

STEPHEN SMITH

ABOVE A beautiful herbal wreath made from fresh botanicals rests atop a terra-cotta urn filled with warty green Osage oranges (or hedge apples). An iron espalier is loaded with more Osage oranges. This piece can be used year-round, both indoors and outdoors, and can be enhanced seasonally with citrus fruits, eggplants, gourds, and even birds' nests.

191

RIGHT The base of this opulent yet natural wreath features bleached antlers and is perfect for the robin's eggs color scheme, which coordinates impressively with natural elements such as pine cones and lichen nests.

OPPOSITE PAGE Distinctive vessels, like these rustic wire urns, are natural displayers for collections of trendy design elements and it's easy to create contemporary compositions.

OPPOSITE PAGE Although tufts of beautiful lavender *Hydrangeas* punctuate this circular "garden," it is the evergreens, in a distinctive range of textures and colors that are the focus. The alluring combination includes berried juniper, silver fir, white pine, golden Japanese cedar (*Cryptomeria*), miniature *Eucalyptus*, and *Berzelia*. The floral foam wreath form on which the centerpiece is created is banded with wire netting in several places for support, and it is those places on which the dramatic two-tone pillar candles are securely positioned.

STEPHEN SMITH

LEFT When wrapped around the rims of painted clay pots, and other types of containers, too, strands of colorful beads create original "jewel"-encrusted vessels. The hand-painted Slavic Santa is recreated from an antique ice-cream mold.

Della Robbia

OPPOSITE PAGE Into a ready-made permanent boxwood wreath, an "orchard-full" of realistic crab apples is glued. A two-loop, navy-checked cotton bow is artfully tucked below the wreath's center.

LEFT Quick and easy to create, these delightful arrangements are just what are called for during holiday times. Pliable, fruit-laden *Cotoneaster* branches are simply wrapped around the necks of the glass vases, and permanent apples and pine cones are arranged just inside and atop the openings of the gold, matte-finished containers. The vases can be filled with excelsior to conserve decorative materials. These fruited branch-wrapped vases are also lovely when filled with potpourri, small glass ornaments, or even pillar candles.

OPPOSITE PAGE Red and gold create an ornate display bursting with the joy of Christmas. This display has a traditional look, with a wreath of ornaments and permanent berries that coordinates with trees of mixed berries fashioned on foam cone forms. Jeweled and glittered trees are also shown, mixed among antique-gold containers. Traditional St. Nicholas figurines clutching candleholders make popular collectibles for Christmas.

STEPHEN SMITH

ABOVE Imparting a splash of holiday color, appropriate for any décor from country comfortable to slick contemporary and even Asian, a stack of square, red, hardwood charger plates frame a grouping of permanent pomegranates, creating a modern piece of art.

OPPOSITE PAGE Inviting guests to enter, a handmade evergreen wreath is adorned with herbs, berries, and fruits. The wreath is designed into a floral foam wreath form and, intendedly so, serves as a food source for birds that nest outdoors during the winter months.

LEFT Glued into a standard vinyl pine tree, a collection of beaded fruit—plums, oranges, lemons, and apples—along with berry sprays and foliage, form a grand tabletop tree with subtle, nonglitsy opulence and Southern refinement.

RIGHT A ready-made wreath ring of fruits and leaves gets a full and customized look with the simple addition of dried cockscomb (*Celosia*) and pods, which are hot-glued into the ring. A short pillar candle completes the full, compact design.

STEPHEN SMITH

STEPHEN SMITH

LEFT & OPPOSITE PAGE Filled with permanent pomegranates, crab apples, and poppy pods, these red-stained, hardwood bowls have wide-ranging appeal. Permanent deciduous and fruited vines encircle the contents and hold them in place. A single shiny glass ornament in each bowl subtly fortifies the Christmas spirit while distinguishing the designs from more traditional collections of fruit.

Commanding attention in a homey setting of provincial goods is an exquisite fruit-laden "topiary." Stacked and glued inside a cone-shaped wire form are permanent apples and preserved pomegranates. Befitting the theme, permanent garden roses bloom among the apples in a rustic bulb tray.

STEPHEN SMITH

Spray-paint a terra-cotta pot gold, and hot-glue in uniform twigs, filling the pot and forming a trunk.

Tie the twigs near the top with florist's twine, and hot-glue a piece of floral foam to the top of the twig trunk.

Add permanent foliage, dried pomegranates, preserved ming fern, and ribbon to finish the design.

A regal arrangement of dried pomegranates, berried branches, and shimmering ribbon rests atop a bundle of twigs, uniform in length and straightness, in this elegant holiday design. The twigs form a sturdy base for the dry floral foam, which is glued on top of the bundle. A low-key container, like this gold pot, completes the look without drawing attention away from the arrangement.

RIGHT Bursting with color and textural variety, this tabletop tree features an eclectic mix of permanent leaves, beads, and even grapes. A foam cone, which is secured atop a salmon-colored flared ceramic pot, is wrapped with sheet moss to create a traditional green base, but the rest of the tree is anything but traditional. Assorted sizes of plastic beads, both spherical and disc shaped, are secured among red corsage leaves and hard plastic leaf ornaments using pearl-headed corsage pins of all colors. In addition to the beads, adding a less expensive dimension to the tree, permanent grapes are separated from clusters and pierced with corsage pins to hold them in place. This novel use of grape clusters offers a reddish-purple jewel-tone beaded look while giving the tree a fruity flair. Decorative wires, in teal and fuchsia, swirl around the finished tree, which is topped with a sleek, shapely teal-blue ornament.

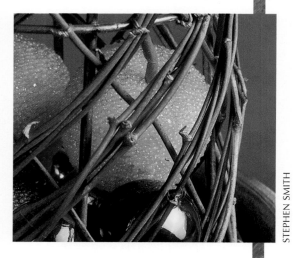

ABOVE & OPPOSITE PAGE
Voguish and wildly popular glass mosaic accessories like the pieces of fruit included here (mosaic vases are also hot) are the perfect decoratives to feature with beaded and "sugared" fruits that are so great with this festive Bohemian theme.

STEPHEN SMITH

STEPHEN SMITH

Glittering Gold

STEPHEN SMITH

Old-world ambience and classic themes are created with the most current of materials. An elegantly detailed adult angel, the antithesis of playful "Victorian" cherubs, is the centerpiece of the display. A classic urn and a pot decorated with Michelangelo-inspired art are filled with contemporary, traditionally nonholiday floral materials. The ambience of the setting is traditional, but the accessories are totally today.

LEFT This unusual design is a new take on the topiary form. A moss-covered square column and sphere rise above an aged pot decorated with gold *Eucalyptus* leaves. Gold bullion and preserved *Eucalyptus* float around the top of the column. Permanent *Eucalyptus* also trails from inverted gold tussie mussie holders attached to the top of the foam column.

how-to
holiday kissing ball

Cover a plastic foam ball with a gold ribbon of your choice. Then, hot-glue permanent holly leaves randomly to the ribbon-covered ball.

Attach a long loop of ribbon to the top of the ball, as a hanger, with a Dixon pin. Secure the insertion with hotglue.

To finish, hot-glue permanent flowers and ribbon streamers to the area where the hanger attaches to the ball.

STEPHEN SMITH

A kissing ball is created with a sheer gold ribbon and holly leaves covering a plastic foam sphere. Another ribbon, the middle of which has a green strip of trees, acts as a decorative hanging device. Permanent flowers and foliage accent this creation, which also may be used as an oversized ornament or a decorative tabletop piece surrounded by smaller ornaments.

Three widths of ribbon act as decorative bands around candles placed in faux vintage antique pots. A wide gold hologram ribbon and a sheer champagne ribbon with a gold striped edge encircle both candles. Delicate antique gold ribbon, 1/8 inch wide, cascades from a wreath of fabric *Hydrangea* blossoms and berry clusters on one candle, and the ribbon forms a swag beneath a band of antique holly on the other.

OPPOSITE PAGE A magnificent 11-foot-tall oak-framed mirror is adorned with an opulent wreath of fresh and dried materials. Suspended from the mirror's frame with luxurious gold, tasseled cording, the wreath, which is crafted from gathered vines, features fresh florals arranged into a bouquet holder, the handle of which is secured among the vines as well as into conical Victorian ornaments that cascade from the wreath.

LEFT Vibrant tones of gold and copper give this wreath a look that is truly modern. Although gold has always paired well with other colors such as red and green, it is perhaps even more striking on its own or with other metallics, especially with the sleek and textured metallic mouth-blown European-style glass ornaments that cover the PVC-based wreath. Lots of berries and *Acanthus* leaves around the edges add the finishing touches to this dazzling creation.

how-to
ribbon-wrapped vase

(see opposite page)

Wrap a cylinder vase with a decorative holiday ribbon, and secure the ribbon to the vase by wrapping it with wired twine or cord.

Cut a cardboard disk that is slightly larger than the top of the cylinder. Cover it with matching ribbon, and secure the ribbon, with hot glue, on the underside of the disk.

Wrap a millimeter ball with wired twine to look like a Christmas bulb, and hot-glue it to the top of the disk. Finish with holly leaves, berries, and millimeter balls.

STEPHEN SMITH

Rife with textural interplay, this casually styled woodsy arrangement of silver-backed *Banksia* foliage *(B. integrifolia)* and fruited *Cotoneaster* branches is dressed for the holidays with gold ornaments, dried poppy pods, and beaded permanent pomegranates. The matte finish of the accents repeats that of the square metal container, creating a unified design. Because of the longevity of the fresh materials, this arrangement could beautify homes and offices from before Thanksgiving well into the Christmas season.

A wide, finely detailed sheer gold ribbon with gold swirls, holly leaves, and three-dimensional "berries" creates a festive display. In addition to covering two cylinders, the ribbon overlays two cardboard discs, one used as the base of an ornament "bud vase" holding red carnations, and one used as a lid for a tall cylinder, which may hold candy, potpourri, or ornaments. Red millimeter balls pick up the red bead accent of the ribbon in each piece.

OPPOSITE PAGE Spectacular and totally innovative, this glittering Christmas composition showcases a pleasing blend of rustic and opulent elements. On a wreath formed of wild branches, shiny gold ornaments are arranged among gold-leafed grapes, oversized matte gold acorns, and frosty permanent grape leaves. And the casual placement of the design, on one upright of a ladder-back chair, is an ingenious way to display the piece and add a holiday highlight to an antique furnishing.

LEFT A stunning combination of gold and copper fruit and foliage, both metallic and matte, produces a tabletop tree with classic elegance. The plastic foam cone, covered with pomegranates; pears; apples; and leaves of oak, *Magnolia*, and holly, is situated atop a Corinthian column candleholder.

how-to
ornamental topiary

Fill a pot with dry floral foam or plastic foam and hot-glue a round ornament directly to the foam. Next, wrap a lichen-covered ball with gold beading wire in a random crisscross pattern.

Hot-glue a finial-shaped ornament to the lichen ball. When the glue has cooled and hardened, hot-glue that two-piece unit to the top of the ornament in the pot.

Hot-glue a ruffled edging of sheer ribbon around the base of the bottom ornament to cover the foam. Also hot-glue a flourish of ribbon between the top and middle ornaments.

STEPHEN SMITH

OPPOSITE PAGE Cut to lengths that are equal to the circumferences of the vases and sprayed with heavy-duty adhesive, pieces of sheer metallic ribbon are attached to glass cylinders at random levels. This inventive technique results in a glimmery essence that gives everyday containers a glamorous holiday look.

ABOVE Repetition is a key element to this affordable yet classy topiary. Although the shapes of the top and bottom ornaments are different, their similar design creates rhythm, as does the repetition of ruffled gold ribbons tacked underneath each glittered ornament. A lichen sphere wrapped with gold beading wire links the top and bottom ornaments. A gold-leafed terra-cotta pot provides a totally different texture yet repeats the metallic features of the ornaments. The aged gold-leaf finish on the pot is achieved by spraying metallic paint onto the surface of water in a bucket, then dipping the pot in it several times to allow the paint to adhere to the pot's surface.